Animals
to the
Rescue

Place: England

Date: April 1998

The Gumbley family was asleep when
a fire started downstairs.

Megan Gumbley's pet rat, Fido, climbed up
15 stairs to scratch at Megan's door.

Then Megan saw the fire!

Fido had saved Megan and her family.

Place: United States

Date: September 2001

Omar Rivera is blind. He was working in the Twin Towers in New York with his guide dog, Salty. Suddenly, a plane crashed into the building. Omar could not run, but he wanted to save Salty. "Go, Salty," he said.

Salty was awarded the Dickin Medal for bravery.

ANIMAL HEROES

Contents

Helen Chapman

Story illustrated by
Carl Pearce

Heinemann

Find out about

- Animals which have saved people's lives and become heroes

Tricky words

- climbed
- building
- pouch
- daughters
- lifeguard
- dolphins
- circle
- horizon
- tsunami

Introduce these tricky words and help the reader when they come across them later!

Text starter

In the Twin Towers disaster in New York, a guide dog saved his owner. In New Zealand, seven dolphins saved some lifeguards from a Great White shark. In the tsunami in Thailand, a baby elephant saved a girl. These are all true stories about animal heroes.

Omar was left alone in the fire and smoke.
Just then, he felt something by his leg.
It was Salty! He had come back for Omar.
Salty led Omar down 71 flights of stairs.
It took them one and a half hours! They
got out just before the building fell down.
Salty had saved his master.

Place: Australia

Date: September 2003

Lulu the kangaroo had been a family pet since Len Richards had found her in the pouch of her mother, who had been killed by a car.

There was a terrible storm, and Len was checking everything was safe on his farm when a branch fell on him and knocked him out.

Lulu stood over Len to keep him safe.
She started barking! Len's family heard a
strange noise. They followed the noise and
found Lulu standing by Len's body.
Nobody even knew that Lulu could bark.
But her barking saved Len's life!

Place: New Zealand

Date: November 2004

Rob Howes, his daughter and her two friends, all lifeguards, were swimming 100 metres from the shore. Suddenly, seven dolphins appeared and began to swim around them in a tight circle. Then Rob saw why – a Great White shark!

The shark was just two metres away. For 40 minutes, the dolphins slapped the water with their tails to keep the shark away from the lifeguards. At last, the shark swam away and the lifeguards were safe. The dolphins had saved their lives.

Place: Thailand

Date: December 2004

Amber Mason was on holiday with her family in Thailand. Amber loved riding into the sea on the back of the tame baby elephant, Ning-Nong, led by her trainer. Suddenly, Ning-Nong stopped.

Ning-Nong's trainer tried to make her go on, but she wouldn't. Then he saw that the waves were being sucked backwards into the sea, and on the horizon he saw a huge wave racing towards them.
He jumped on Ning-Nong's back with Amber and they rushed to the shore.

The huge wave was caused by an under sea earthquake. A wave like this is called a "tsunami". This tsunami crashed on to the shore and dragged thousands of people out to sea.

Somehow, Ning-Nong had known about the danger and that is why she would not go on into the sea.

Five minutes before the huge waves hit, other elephants working near a village did something strange. They all suddenly stopped and stood still. Then they turned and ran up a nearby hill. When the people saw this, they ran after the elephants. Minutes later, the huge waves hit the village.

The elephants had saved the people's lives.

All of these animals saved people's lives.
They are all heroes.
Do you have a pet? Has it ever done anything brave? Would it save your life?
Perhaps it could be a pet hero too!

Quiz

Text Detective

- How did Megan's pet rat save her and her family?
- Which animal do you think was bravest?

Word Detective

- Phonic Focus: Unstressed vowels
  Page 6: Which letter represents the unstressed vowel in 'terrible'? (i)
- Page 9: Find a word that means 'hit'.
- Page 13: What sound does the 'ed' make at the end of 'stopped'?

Super Speller

Read these words:

family   terrible   strange

Now try to spell them!

HA! HA! HA!

Q How do elephants stay in touch?

A By elephone!

In this story

 Karl

Adam

 Lizzie,
a burglar

 Rick,
another burglar

Tricky words

- spread
- chew
- wires
- raisins
- settled
- whispered
- squeaked
- sweat

Introduce these tricky words and help the reader when they come across them later!

Story starter

Karl and Adam were best friends. It was Karl's birthday and he had been given a pet rat as a present. Adam thought the rat was a strange present, but he was in for a surprise!

Rats Rule!

"Look out, Karl!" said Adam. "It's a rat!"
Adam backed away slowly.

"I know it's a rat!" said Karl. "It's my birthday present. His name is Pip."

"Oh," said Adam. "Silly me, I bought you this DVD for your birthday. I could have just looked in the gutter for a rat!"

"No one likes rats, I don't know why," said Karl.

"I know why," said Adam. "They spread germs and ... "

"Not this one," said Karl.

"They chew through wires," said Adam.

"Not this one," said Karl.

"Do you want to bet?" said Adam, holding up the wire from the DVD player. It was chewed into two bits!

"Oh no!" said Karl. "Look at the mess Pip has made! He's chewed holes in lots of boxes of food, too. Mum will be mad when she gets back."

"He must have chewed into a box of chocolate raisins," said Adam.

"They're all over the floor."

"They're not raisins," said Karl.

"That's rat poo!"

"Oh yuk!" said Adam.

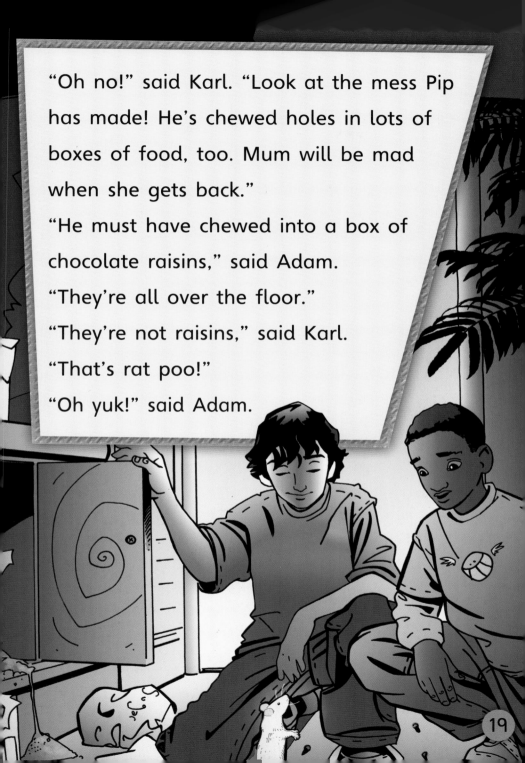

"We'll have to watch the DVD at my house," said Adam.

"OK," said Karl. "I'll just give Pip his food." He cut up a banana and put it in Pip's food bowl. Then he and Adam went out. Pip ate the banana, then he settled down for a little sleep.

Later that evening, the window slowly opened. A torch lit up the room as a girl climbed in.

"It's OK, Rick," she said. "No one's here." She put on the light. "You grab the TV and DVD player. I'm going to look for money and credit cards."

Pip was still asleep. They didn't see him.

"Look, Lizzie!" said Rick. "Chocolate raisins! They're everywhere! My favourite!"

"Forget the raisins," said Lizzie. "We're here to rob the place, not to eat."

She picked up Karl's wallet and mobile and put them in her pocket.

"Get that laptop and CD player and put them in the car."

"But I'm hungry," said Rick.

When Lizzie wasn't looking, Rick picked up some raisins. He tossed them into his mouth. At once he knew he'd made a bad mistake.

"AAARGH!" he screamed as he spat them out. "They're disgusting!"

Just then, Karl and Adam came back. They heard the noise.

"Mum must be back," said Karl. He looked through the living room window.

"Quick, give me your phone," he whispered.

"What's up?" asked Adam.

"Robbers," said Karl as he called the police.

"Come on – we can watch through the living room window."

Just then, Pip woke up. He could see the robbers. Pip didn't like strangers.
He puffed up his fur and hissed, but the strangers didn't leave. Pip squeaked, then he leaped ... and landed on Lizzie's head!

Pip's claws and sharp teeth dug into Lizzie's nose.

"Ow!" she yelled. "Yuk, it's a rat – kill it!"

"Oh no!" whispered Karl. "Don't kill Pip!"

But then they watched in surprise as Pip took charge.

Pip ran down Lizzie's body. Then he ran across the floor and on to Rick's foot. He crept inside Rick's baggy jeans and ran up his leg!

Rick froze with fear. Sweat dripped down his face. "Lizzie," he cried. "Do something! I **hate** rats!"

Pip bit Rick's knee.

"Ouch!" Rick cried, hopping on one leg. "It's bitten me!"

"Quick, take off your jeans," said Lizzie.

Rick pulled down his jeans and made a grab for Pip. But he tripped and crashed on to the floor.

Karl and Adam couldn't help it – they both started to laugh!

Rick spun round. "Who's there?" he shouted.

He saw Karl and Adam at the window. "Right," he yelled. "You're for it!"

Karl and Adam looked at each other. "What now?" said Adam.

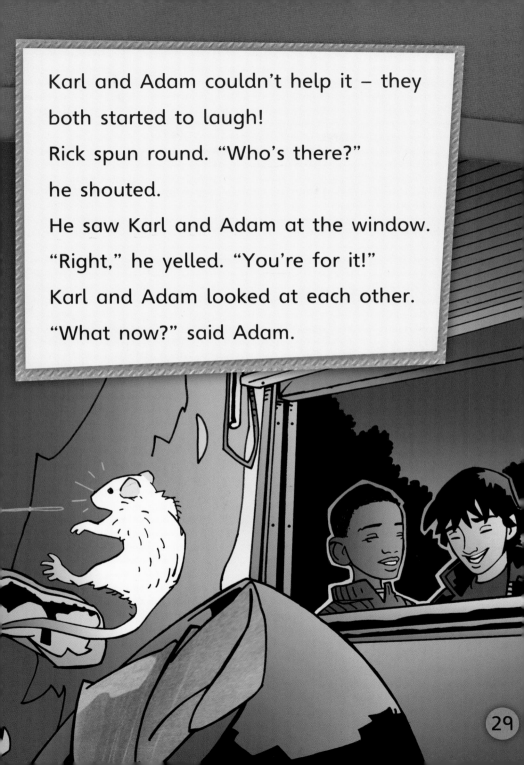

Just then, they heard a car driving up. They spun round. It was a police car! Two police officers jumped out. They ran into the house and found Rick and Lizzie with all the gear.

"Right, you two," said the officers.

"You're nicked!"

Later, Karl and Adam told the police what had happened.

"That's one clever rat," said a police officer. "I thought they were all pests."

"No one likes rats," said Adam as he petted Pip. "I don't know why!"

"Well, he's a hero," said the officer, as he popped a chocolate raisin into his mouth.

Quiz

Text Detective

- What did the policeman eat?
- Do you think Pip is a hero?

Word Detective

- **Phonic Focus:** Unstressed vowels
  Page 17: Which letters represent the unstressed vowel in 'gutter'? (er)
- Page 25: Find a word meaning 'took a big jump'.
- Page 27: Why is the word 'hate' in bold?

Super Speller

Read these words:

screamed   bought   evening

Now try to spell them!

HA! HA! HA!

 Why do policemen need to be strong?

So they can hold up the traffic.